SHARKS

New and Updated

by Gail Gibbons

HOLIDAY HOUSE · NEW YORK

Special thanks to Robert Hueter and Kerry Kirschner
of Mote Marine Laboratory, Sarasota, Florida

Special thanks also to Barbara Brown and Radford Arrindell,
of the Ichthyology Department, American Museum of Natural History

HOLIDAY HOUSE is registered in the U.S. Patent and Trademark Office.
Printed and bound in September 2019 at Tien Wah Press, Johor Bahru, Johor, Malaysia.
www.holidayhouse.com
Second Edition
1 3 5 7 9 10 8 6 4 2

Library of Congress has catalogued the prior edition as follows:

Library of Congress Cataloging-in-Publication Data

Gibbons, Gail.
Sharks / by Gail Gibbons.
p.   cm.
Summary: Describes shark behavior and different kinds of sharks.
ISBN 0-8234-0960-0
1. Sharks—Juvenile literature. [1. Sharks.] I. Title.
QL638.9.G383   1992   91-31524   CIP   AC
597'.31—dc20

ISBN 978-0-8234-4571-4 (hardcover)
ISBN 978-0-8234-1068-2 (paperback)

Sharks live in oceans and fresh water. They are fish. There are more than 500 different kinds of sharks.

There are small sharks, big sharks, and . . .

huge sharks!

CARCHAROCLES (car•CAR•o•clees) **MEGALODON** was about 43 feet long. *Carcharodon* means "rough tooth." *Megalodon* means "giant tooth." It had very sharp teeth about eight inches long.

The first sharks lived more than 400 million years ago, 200 million years before dinosaurs walked the earth. Most of them were only about 3 feet long. Later, sharks grew to be bigger. Some were enormous. One of them was *Carcharocles megalodon*.

The **CAUDAL FIN** pushes the shark forward when it is moved back and forth.

DORSAL FIN

SECOND DORSAL FIN

ANAL FIN

PELVIC FINS

The **PECTORAL FINS** balance and lift the shark.

DENTICLES (DENT•i•culs)

Sharks are not like other fish. Fish have smooth scales. Sharks' bodies are covered with scales called denticles that have sharp little teeth in them. Most fish skeletons are made of bone. Shark skeletons are not made of bone but of a softer elastic material called cartilage.

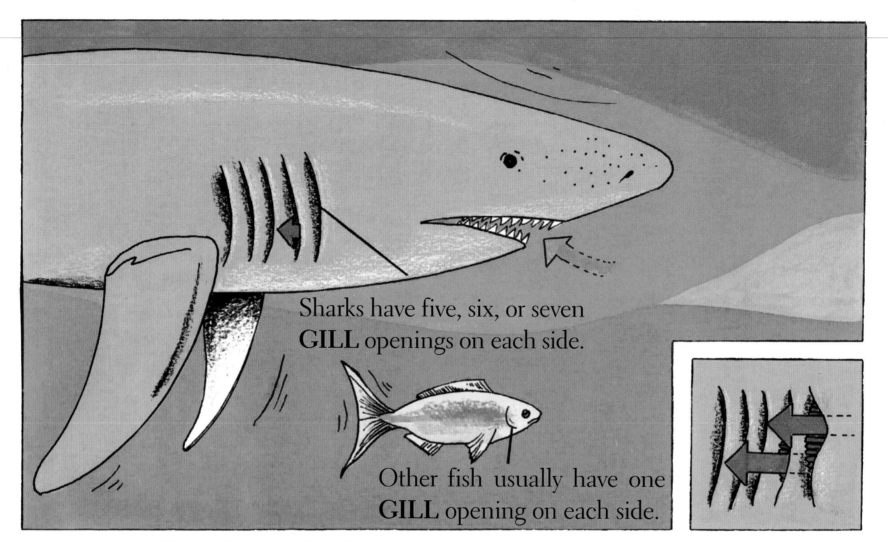

Sharks have five, six, or seven **GILL** openings on each side.

Other fish usually have one **GILL** opening on each side.

Sharks breathe by drawing water into their mouths as they swim. When the water passes the gills, it touches small blood vessels. These blood vessels take the oxygen from the water to keep the sharks alive. Unlike other fish, many sharks must keep moving to make the water flow over their gills.

LATERAL LINE ORGANS

Sharks have sharp senses that work together. They have inner ears. Their ears are tubes running under their skin to their skulls. They can hear distant sounds, even a heartbeat. On the sides of their bodies are small canals under their skin called lateral line organs. They are sensitive to movement in the water and can help guide the shark to what is moving.

AMPULLAE
(AM•pew•lee)

Sharks can use electricity to hunt, too. All living creatures in the water give off small electrical signals. Sharks have tiny holes in their faces called ampullae. They pick up the signals that guide the sharks in the right direction. Sharks also have a very good sense of smell. They can tell the direction a smell is coming from, sometimes a mile away.

Sharks' eyes are sensitive to light. They can see things underwater where light is often dim.

Sharks don't use their teeth for chewing. They use their teeth to tear, bite, and crush food. Most sharks have more than four rows of teeth. Their front teeth do all the work. When a shark loses a tooth, it will soon be replaced by a new one.

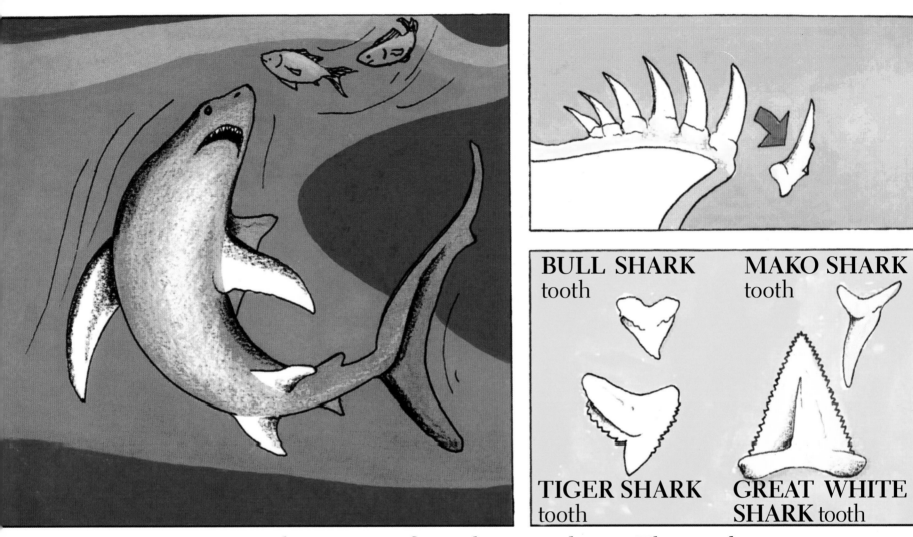

New teeth move up from the second row. They replace worn out or missing teeth in the front row. The teeth in the third and fourth rows move forward, too. Different sharks have teeth that are different sizes and shapes.

EGG

Shark babies are born two ways. Some sharks lay tough, thorny-cased eggs on or near the bottom of the ocean. It takes a few weeks before the baby sharks chew their way out of the egg cases and swim away.

PUP

Other sharks develop from eggs inside the mother's body. Usually it takes about 6 months to 2 years before these babies are born alive. Shark babies can care for themselves from the minute they are born. They are called pups.

Most sharks are not dangerous. Of the over 500 kinds of sharks, only about 30 species have been known to attack people. This rarely happens. When it does, it usually is because the shark has mistaken the movement of a person for the movement of a fish or something else it is hunting.

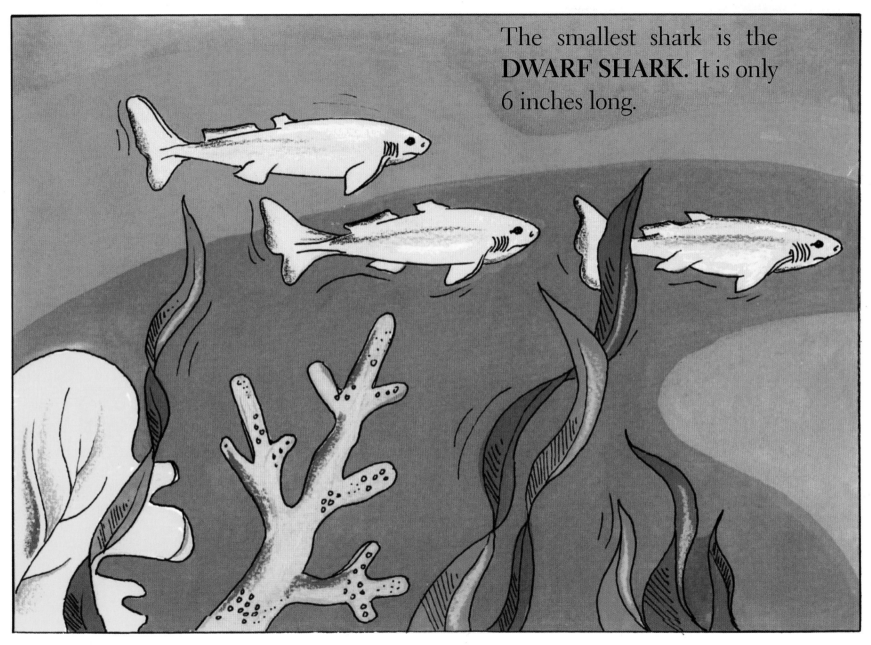

The smallest shark is the **DWARF SHARK.** It is only 6 inches long.

Sharks are different shapes and sizes.

BULL SHARKS are about 10 feet long. They are fierce and aggressive. They've been known to attack people who are swimming. Bull sharks are one of only two kinds of shark that can live in fresh water. On rare occasions they are spotted swimming in rivers.

BLUE SHARKS usually live in deep waters. They migrate thousands of miles to have their babies and search for new food.

MAKO SHARKS can be up to 11 feet long and can swim as fast as 43 miles an hour! They can be dangerous.

TIGER SHARKS can grow up to 24 feet long. They are often found in shallow water. Tiger sharks eat fish, seabirds, crabs, turtles, and even smaller sharks. They are one of the most dangerous sharks.

The **THRESHER SHARK** can be up to 20 feet long. It has a very long, powerful tail, which it uses to stun prey. It eats small fish and usually doesn't bother people.

NURSE SHARKS often hide in underwater caves and reefs for long periods of time. They have strong, blunt teeth. They eat fish, shrimp, lobster, sea urchins, and crabs.

HAMMERHEAD SHARKS can be almost 20 feet long and are strange looking. Their heads are flat and shaped like a double-headed hammer. They eat fish, squid, crabs, and stingrays. Hammerhead sharks live in shallow, warm waters and have been known to attack people.

GREAT WHITE SHARKS
are famous for being the most dangerous and fiercest members of the shark family. They will eat large fish, other sharks, and even whales.

They have very strong jaws and hundreds of teeth, sometimes three inches long. Each tooth has a sharp, jagged edge like a saw blade.

The **BASKING SHARK** is very large and can grow to be about 40 feet long. It is slow moving and generally harmless. It eats small animals and plant life called plankton.

The **BASKING SHARK** likes to swim near the surface of the water, sometimes in large groups.

The **WHALE SHARK** is the biggest fish that ever existed. It can be 60 feet long and weigh up to 15 tons. Although it is very strong and powerful, it eats only plankton and small fish.

The **WHALE SHARK** never attacks people or even large fish. It swims slowly and lazily, usually just below the surface of the water.

For many years sharks have been fished and hunted by people. Before sandpaper was invented, people used shark skin to smooth and polish wood. Some Native American nations used sharp, hard shark teeth for arrowheads. Others used shark teeth for jewelry.

Today, in some places, shark skin is used to make shoes, purses, and belts. Also, shark meat is used for food. There is sport fishing, too. Some species have been fished and hunted to the point where there is concern about their survival.

Sharks play an important role, like all other ocean life. It is good to protect these mysterious and marvelous creatures and the sea in which they live.

Scientists and people can learn a lot from studying sharks.
To know about sharks is to admire and respect them.

The whale shark lays the world's biggest egg. It is about 12 inches long!

The whale shark has skin thicker than any other creature's. It is up to 6 inches thick.

The dot pattern on a whale shark's back is unique, like a human fingerprint, and can be used by scientists to identify them.

A person is more likely to be killed by lightning or a bee sting than by a shark.

IMPORTANT ...

If you see a shark when you are swimming ...

Slowly swim away from the shark toward the shore or boat.

Remain calm. Don't shout or splash.

Remember, you are in the shark's world. Don't swim toward the shark.

The chances are the shark isn't interested in you and will swim away.

If you are around other people when you reach the shore or boat, tell someone in authority what you saw so other swimmers can be notified.